MW01609022

MY TWO BITS' WORTH

Hi Judy,

A member of the older generation trying to be a poet. If it doesn't measure up just consider the source.

Stanley Anderson

MY TWO BITS' WORTH

Stanley Allan Anderson

VANTAGE PRESS
New York

All illustrations are by Jan Akin, except for those on pages 15, 21, 26, 38, and 99, which are by Lola Anderson.

All biblical quotations are taken from the Revised Standard Version and New International Version of the Bible.

Published by Vantage Press, Inc.
516 West 34th Street, New York, New York 10001

Manufactured in the United States of America
ISBN: 0-533-11850-6

Library of Congress Catalog Card No.: 95-91024

0 9 8 7 6 5 4 3 2 1

To my mother, who has a great love for poetry

Contents

Foreword

The quarter, or two bit piece, as it is commonly called, has the words "Liberty" and "In God We Trust" inscribed on its face and, by virtue of the head of George Washington also inscribed, the word "Patriotism" is inferred. These three virtues reflect what this author considers the true values of life. It is his hope that the offerings in this book reflect those values, with a little humor thrown in to spice them up.

MY TWO BITS' WORTH

Puget Sound Country

Were I to travel the whole world round
In search of the perfect location,
In my mind's eye I would say Puget Sound
Is the most favored place in creation.

With an inland sea and an exquisite land
Banked by spruce, hemlock, and fir,
To which the great artist with brush in hand,
Added myriad colors to the stir;

Rhododendrons, wild flowers, and reddish madronnas,
Shadow of uplands in the waters below,
Tall peaks in the distance like hallowed madonnas,
Glistening white with the winter's snow.

From Tatoosh to Point Roberts, to Tumwater Falls,
Traversing the channels of Puget Sound,
Perhaps sighting the orcas one's heart enthralls
To see them leaping and cavorting around.

And emerald isles in an intriguing maze
Inviting the adventuresome to explore;
To sail the San Juans is to feast one's gaze
On majestic mountains and island shore.

Then the Hood Canal with its fiordlike arm
Harboring sandy beaches and forest glade,
To the bordering peninsulas it lands its charm,
No more enchanting place hath God ever made.

How fertile its water as it ebbs and flows
Baring tidelands and shells by the shore;
Home of seagulls, herons, and scavenging crows,
Nurturing spawn of smelt and oyster spore.

It's a gentle land with climate mild
And a landscape so fresh and clean,
Cleaned by rain and sun and pampered child,
'Tis called the land of the evergreen.

Wind

No person knows the path of the wind.
It blows when and wherever it pleases.
So frisky, frolicsome, and undisciplined,
Who would tame it, it plays with and teases.

As it swishes by with a roar or a sigh,
You feel its presence but yet it's unseen.
One cannot take hold of this passerby;
It's unrestrained like a free libertine.

The whole earth the playground of this vagabond,
A loyal partner in cahoots with the sun.
When the sun waves its wand, the wind does respond
By rising up and taking off on a run.

It runs o'er the surface searching for lows,
Where they're found, displaced air will replace.
When each low is found, it puffs and it blows
Until fresh air will have refilled the space.

Then it's up and away to form the jet stream,
Its serpentine pathway splitting the sky,
Or to frighten the earth with fury and scream,
A whirling dervish round the hurricane's eye.

It's so steady, the tradewind, as its plies the sea,
Unless in doldrum depresses sailor and sail,
And it pushes the clouds on their Odyssey
To deliver cargo of rain, snow, or hail.

The unseen wind is nature's most stubborn child,
Yet a good friend to old Mother Earth.
Though it stirs up the earth with antics so wild,
All the good things it does of great worth.

In the heat of the day, Old Sol blazing away,
When all things are in state of prostration,
How grateful the earth for the wind's interplay,
For all nature now revived by aeration.

When winter's cold blast seems forever to last,
And solid ice is frozen over the brook,
How happy the day people hear the forecast:
"There is coming the warm winds of chinook."

When fragrant scents are being born downwind,
And nature's sweets are being sent to allure,
Just watch all the bees, they're so disciplined,
Soon field and garden will be all astir.

How majestic the eagle as it soars on high,
Its eyes scanning the panorama below.
As this scourge of the hunted streaks from the sky,
It rides the winds to deliver death's blow.

How buoyant the wind, where'er it may blow,
A place to play for the seagulls astride her,
Their wings barely flutter against the flow,
But downwind it's free flight like a glider.

One of nature's artists, it sculptures the land,
For millions of years incessantly hewing;
But impatient with dunes it keeps shifting sand,
And drifts of snow is forever renewing.

The surfer rides from the crest of the wave,
But the sailboat glides smooth o'er the sea.
How generous the wind, all the waves that it gave,
All the breezes that have formed them are free.

Gazing out at a field of lush golden grain,
Waving sprightly in the wind and the sun;
Such a beautiful sight did not God so ordain,
That we'd marvel at the things He has done.

Autumn Leaves

It's autumn now and the leaves not yet falling,
Nature's showcase now displaying its ware
Like music's crescendo it sets for enthralling,
Brilliant colors are unfurled everywhere.

Down in the valley or up on the hillside,
Wherever maples or oaks choose to dwell,
Or any kind of tree where it may reside
Will join forces to on you cast a spell.

For your eyes now bedazzled by shades of color,
Such as browns, golds, yellows, and vermilions;
Others scarlet of hue, but some a bit duller,
Such profusion the leaves number in billions.

As always is so in nature's grand story,
Before it sleeps through the long night of winter,
Its last hurrah is this blaze of glory;
For lasting image this will serve as imprinter.

For nature is anxious that you not forget,
That after winter comes renewal of spring.
Then leaves come again to expectancy whet
For fall colors that'll again be emblazoning.

The Cove

Who will ever forget the charm of that cove,
With each new day's offerings a treasure trove
Of beautiful scenes on one's mind to be etched,
To say it can spellbind is not too farfetched.

To look out one's window at scenes ever changing,
Mother Nature forever at work rearranging;
Perhaps one day white caps, the next sea of calm,
The water so roiled put at ease by her balm.

As you witness the tide with its ebb and flow,
Surely man in the moon has great pull below,
When he ebbs the tide, mud denizens scurry,
But reversing to flow, there's no need to hurry.

In the midst of the night the moon shining above,
Its beams shimmer on water is as light-o-love
So entrancing the soul one reluctant to leave,
Fearing once the scene lost, one cannot retrieve.

In the time of the freeze, perhaps month of January,
How amusing the ducks in their winter sanctuary,
One moment in view, then a vanishing act
As they dive for the bottom to some goody extract.

How exciting the days when the smelt start to run,
Throwing caution to wind, they no longer shun
The sand on the shore where to lay egg and sperm
Where birth of their babies will soon come to term.

In the day of a storm the wind and waves raging,
So spectacular the show that nature's now staging
As wild white-capped waves race for the shore,
Where they'll crash on the rocks to be seen no more.

In time for sport be it swimming or sailing,
Or people on skis in their wild ride regaling,
Or the fisherman tensed to bring in a fish;
To watch people's joy, what more could one wish?

So fertile its water, the sound teeming with life,
Death and life struggles before one are rife,
Starfish on oyster or the seal cruising through,
And seagull or heron searching food to pursue.

But to walk on the beach is to explore to the full
The rocks and shells, which are so bountiful,
To see a clam squirt its hiding place to reveal,
Or see the crabs scamper, which seems so unreal.

But above all the wonders it has a mystique
As far shore through the mist plays hide and seek,
Or to see upland shadows reflected in water;
Among wonders of nature, this a most favored daughter.

The Sentinel

All over that area it was barren and flat;
No protrusion not even tree broke the view.
But a huge old rock dwelled in that habitat,
It was a mystery where it dwelled hitherto.

Twice the height of an outhouse it stood alone;
The march of time had settled it in a nest.
It looked so mysterious, it was a lodestone,
In this setting it loomed up as Mount Everest.

So out of place one could not help wonder
How such a phenomenon as this could occur.
From some jutting crag, was this rent asunder
And here in exile placed by some banisher?

The earliest travelers named it The Sentinel,
Watching over what took place on that flat.
All the happenings thereon too many to tell
But recorded by this lone secretariat.

For here within scope would great dramas unfold
Or tranquil scenes spread before to enchant;
A badger invading a gopher household,
Or red sunset for ecstatic anticipant.

Here too was home of great herds of buffalo,
Huge behemoths spreading out on the plain.
When they were spooked, in mass flight they would go,
But when exhausted from wild flight they'd detrain.

At the base of the rock was a deep-seated trail,
Worn deep by the denizens of the plain
Who rubbed against rock to scratch itchy scale,
As would buffalos and other beasts of domain.

At the top of the rock how inviting a perch,
The birds of prey would alight for a spell.
All about they could see and make careful search
Where any movement would their next meal foretell.

Were it able to speak The Sentinel could tell
About the buffalo hunt and spent arrow;
How deer and antelope in its shadow did dwell,
As did rattlesnake, sage hen, or sparrow.

Always slinking nearby, a fox or a coyote:
All the innocents in usual state of unease.
Those villains ever probing for a snack to promote
With their cunning, the unsuspecting they'd seize.

Down through the ages great onslaughts of nature
Had battered The Sentinel as it stood alone.
Wild storms with wind, heat, and cold to endure,
Nature's ragings couldn't topple that stone.

From time immemorial this rock as a lighthouse
Has been a beacon of which wayfarers tell.
How the terror of lost, which this land did rouse,
Would dissolve when catching sight of The Sentinel.

Living Creatures

Living creatures at home on land, air, or sea,
Infinite are their numbers and design.
The great God created this menagerie
With man the sovereign, His mandate divine.

From tiny amoeba to gargantuan whale
With social order peculiar to each;
Their habits and traits almost seem fairytale,
Like dancing bees or clams digging the beach.

How strange the octopus with its suction-cup arms,
Equipped with funnel to propel itself forward;
Or how human the ants as they tend their farms
With herds of aphids, which they milk under guard.

The browser stretches its neck to top of trees;
It was designed that there it should fare.
The long-necked giraffe can all about oversee
If there be enemies of which to beware.

In the harshest most frigid clime of all
Lives the gregarious waddling penguin.
How strange in a land where few hear its call,
Multiplied thousands create deafening din.

The king of the beasts, a creature so fearsome,
Who reigns supreme and is lord o'er the plain;
When it goes on the prowl it is most worrisome,
For the prey knows it is hungry again.

How marvelous the ultimate flying machine,
Its maneuvers bordering on the absurd;
Flying or hovering, twirling wings barely seen,
It's so mighty, the wee hummingbird.

Prehistoric in look, one of the north's denizen,
Shaggy coat almost touching the ground,
Forming a circle, defense-minded muskoxen
Keep their babies safe within the compound.

The land down under a most unusual zoo
With odd creatures such as platypus and wombat,
But to hop at top speed like pouched kangaroo,
 A tricky feat by this strange acrobat.

See nature's surveyors mark territorial preserves
Such as wolf, or the fox, or the cheetah.
See antics of wildebeest toward foe it unnerves.
Nature's offerings truly all are phenomena.

Consider monarch butterfly, or graceful swallow,
Or the salmon, humped whale, or the turtle.
Whereto they should migrate they seem to foreknow,
How to navigate, God in them, did instill.

Among all these creatures, man's greatest friend,
As this concluded with this epilogue,
Is companion and helper on whom to depend:
His ever faithful and loving dog.

Beachcomber

Like an old prospector searching for gold,
The lone stranger step by step moved along.
His wanderings here and there seemed uncontrolled
Along the shore where the sea sings its song.

As a beachcomber does he cut a wide swath
In search of treasure to claim as his own,
That may have been beached by wild wave and froth;
How thrilling to make a find unforeknown.

One moment pausing at the edge of a ripple
To gaze seaward o'er the waves at a loon,
Then moving to look at a seagull cripple
Before meandering toward shore to a dune.

For he had detected the wind working there,
Shifting sand along front of some driftwood.
With driftwood as backdrop and sculpted with care
A mounded dune glistening white now there stood.

Like a child on the beach he climbed o'er the dune,
Then moved purposely back toward the ocean
To look for the loot that waves may have strewn,
Back and forth the man strode with devotion.

It seemed wave and sand had on him cast a spell,
For persistently he inched ever forward.
The search was the thing, what he'd find hard to tell,
Time and distance could not now pull him shoreward.

An observer perched on a bank on the shore
Looking out at the beachcombing figure,
Could see by his tracks the path to explore,
Though wind and wave would the tracks soon disfigure.

As you ponder the view, isn't life like that,
Every soul like that beachcombing stranger,
Roaming hither and yon seeking treasure whereat,
But sands of time for one's path the deranger.

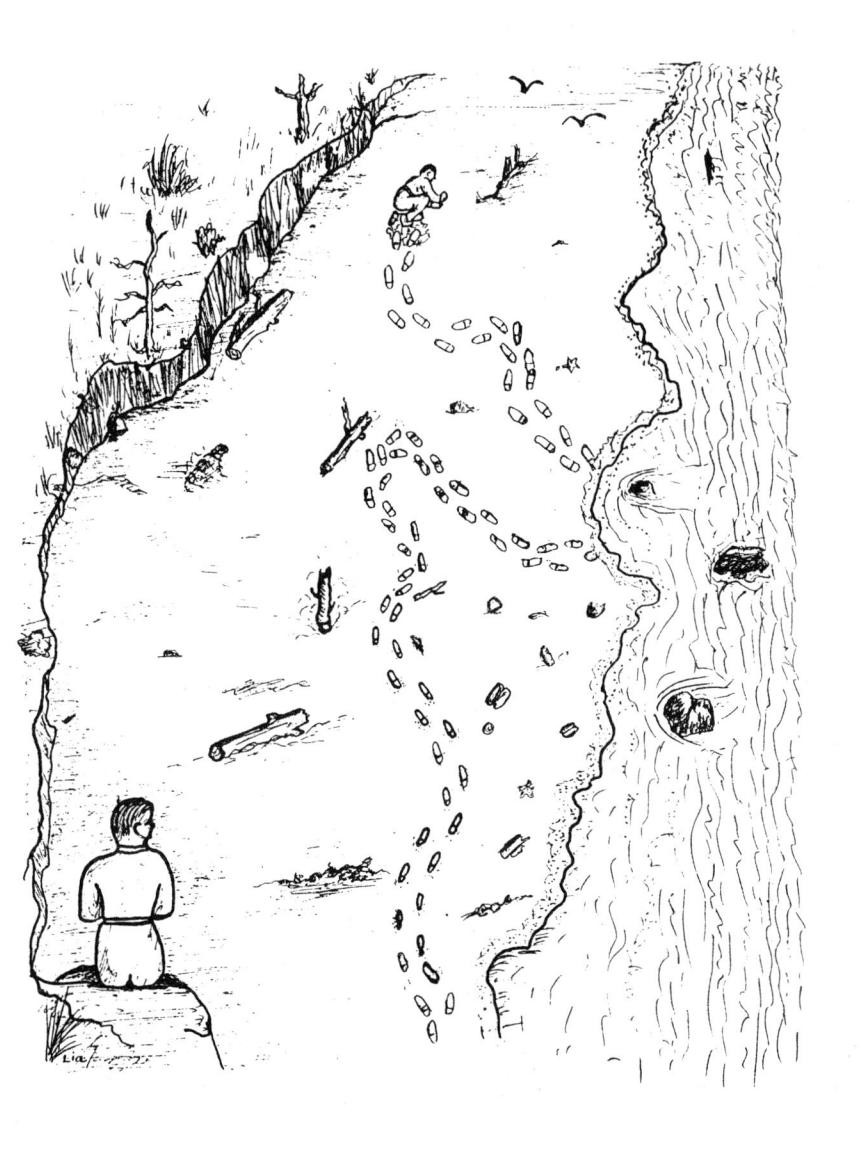

The Gardener

From time of Adam in Garden of Eden,
Born within there seems to be innate yen,
To plant a garden and make something grow,
That on gardeners will fulfillment bestow.

This urge to garden builds up in the spring
When they're anxious to begin this fun thing.
They measure the days and note wind and sun,
And do lament until the job is begun.

Impatience grows to start working the soil,
Won't abate until they feel sweat of toil.
The pleasure will come when wait turns to deed,
When time's ripe to ready ground for the seed.

This is the time gardener's pride enters in,
If row's crooked it will cause them chagrin,
For when the seeds sprout and push through the ground,
There'll be evidence if such rows can be found.

Then will begin many wars to be fought
Against a voracious, relentless juggernaut,
For aphids and worms plus beetle and weevil
Will invade with their wont to do evil.

As gardeners tend growing gardens with care,
They feed and water and eradicate tare.
It's then that wonderment and marvel take hold
As nature's miracles do before them unfold.

It's anticlimactic to taste of the fruit,
'Tis the process that gardeners salute;
That seed in soil sparked by water and sun
Rouses nature to produce such phenomenon.

Dust Devils

On cloudless clear days in heat of summer,
The sun's rays bearing down on the plain,
With dry barren ground now gasping for breath,
It starts a whirlwind for some air to attain.

It's ever on move so ghostlike and playful,
Along hillside or down on the level.
Meandering its path like a top spinning free,
'Tis apparition which we know as dust devil.

In nature's storehouse what more mysterious
Then this erratic, capricious vagabond.
Does some flighty spirit incite its vagary,
As straight it goes, then veers offline beyond?

Fascination will grip even dullest watcher,
As over dry, barren ground it goes whirling,
For it sucks and draws up the dust and debris,
Shoots them upward fast spinning and twirling.

As up they're lofted by vortex impounding,
Unceremoniously they're spewed out of the spin,
To free fall to earth in strange new surrounding,
Where once again will the sun's scorch begin.

Dust devils soon die, for the spin runs down,
Can't be revived until the ground gasps again,
But to liven the earth on a hot summer day,
Will stir again to bring fresh burst of oxygen.

Face to Face

I was busy there by the side of the fence
Taking care of some business at hand,
When out of my eye saw movement commence,
A herd of cattle walking over the land.

While they were grazing they noticed me there,
Being curious they were coming to see.
That I was a stranger they all were aware,
And so purposely came walking toward me.

Now drawing closer they came to a pause,
And all faced me in a semi-curved line.
Then as on cue invisible line they did cross
As curiosity did their fear undermine.

Their steps now hesitant as forward they came,
Though not fearful they were cautious somewhat.
Then within reach necks stretched from their frame,
They sniffed shyly but that was close as they got.

Being intrigued to receive such attention,
I was struck by all that beauty before me.
That cattle so curious I lacked comprehension,
They showed interest in all they could see.

Now more at ease they continued to eye
My every move as I worked at my task,
But those comely faces did my sense occupy,
And while it lasted I continued to bask.

Each face had pattern when more than one color;
The combinations were from black, white, or red,
But all those faces from plain to tricolor
Had magnificence beyond what could be said.

My view now has changed that cattle are dull;
Of beasts of interest they rate a high place.
That off-chance happening seemed like a miracle;
My eyes were opened when we met face to face.

Our Backyard

It is so delightful our backyard setting
With grassy landscape and trees scattered there,
And to add to joy is nature begetting
So many creatures their presence to share.
As one peers through the window in morning
Perhaps a bunny will be hopping slow;
Though alert for any danger forewarning,
It keeps nibbling on the grasses below.

A frequent caller year around is the crow,
A bottomless pit ever scrounging for food;
Hopping and crowfooting they go to and fro,
In choice of menu they will nothing exclude.
Then suddenly the crows will enliven the scene
By stretching necks in a loud raucous call,
Then as black shiny rogues together convene,
They stage a boisterous uninhibited ball.

Among the earliest harbingers of spring
Are robin redbreasts so saucy and pert,
They come swiftly gliding low on the wing,
And immediately pull worms from the dirt.
In all of nature is there more noble sight
Then a robin standing tall in a stare?
When alertly it guards as a medieval knight,
It's the grandest, no other pose can compare.

Other visitors pay respects to our yard,
The noisy bluejay and the wee chick-a-dee,
Feisty hummingbirds have feeders to guard;
There's sapsuckers and the bashful towhee;
And then below the swift streaking swallow
Four-footed creatures come by to enthrall,
The playful otter to the pond to wallow;
Deer and possum will occasionally call.

But most frequent visitors come in the fall;
The squirrels know when it's harvest time.
As they note the chestnuts are ready to haul
They scamper swiftly and agile in climb.
As you watch these bushy-tails hard at work,
So industrious as they bring in the crop,
There's a lesson for man to work and not shirk,
The same diligence should apply in his shop.

Tribute to Mother

A Tribute to My Mother on Her Ninetieth Birthday

What a wonderful mother, that mother of mine. She is old now and her hair is white. She is stooped and her fingers are gnarled from years of hard work. But there is a twinkle in her eye and love shines there. No sourpuss here but a lady of good humor with a laugh so infectious it tickles the funny bone of everyone around her. She is wise too from what God and life have taught her. Joy and thankfulness are in her heart that she was willing way back there at the beginning to accept God's plan for a woman to marry a man, bear children, and to be his helpmate for better or for worse. And worse it was before it got better. Being the wife of a homesteader presented challenge and hardship hard to comprehend. With borrowed money for a team of horses and a twelve-by-fourteen foot homestead shack in which to begin a family, what iron will God must have implanted into the heart of this maiden and that of her husband to be able to withstand the rigors of the harsh Montana prairie as they began their adventure in nineteen-eighteen. Undisturbed sod of millenniums had to be broken up to provide the seed beds for future crops. Comforts and conveniences as we know them today were slow and long in coming. Running water and indoor plumbing could not be afforded for another quarter century. Even so, the home was always scrubbed and clean. The smell of bread baking in the oven will always be savored and the good home cooking that made its way to the table at its appointed time always with good cheer marked this lady as wonderful helpmate and provider for her husband and family. Proverbs says it well. A wife of noble character who can find? She is worth far more than rubies. Her husband has full confidence in her and lacks nothing of value. She brings him good, not harm, all the days of her life. She is clothed with strength and dignity; she can laugh at the days to come. She speaks with wisdom and faithful instruction is on her tongue. She watches over the affairs of her household and does not eat the bread of idleness. Her husband, children, grandchildren, and great-grandchildren rise up and call her blessed. Charm is deceptive and beauty is fleeting, but a woman who fears the Lord is to be praised. Give her the tribute that is her due and let her works bring her praise at the city gate.

MY MOTHER, she is wise. She has chosen "Life in exuberance for Eternity."

A Pearl

Sometimes in His wisdom the Father above
Will pluck from this world by an act of His love
Some lad or lass not passed through childhood.
For those left behind, this is not understood.

She was with us just a little while,
This little girl who showed no guile.
Her face was framed by long blond curls,
This artless one among the girls.

Not one she did not see as friend;
Toward one and all her steps would wend.
All humans were alike to her,
She ranked no one she would prefer.

Her first words, "Hi! How-do-you-do?"
Then searched your face with eyes so blue.
Then cheeks would branch into a smile,
And she would linger for a while.

Her love of life was keen and bold.
She inspected all within its fold:
The flowers, the birds, a ball in park,
On adventure train she'd fast embark.

She'd run and play in utter glee
And then she'd shout for all to see,
"Oh! Look at me, I'm playing too,"
Though no one else she could out-do.

For nature played a cruel trick;
When giving bodies tossed her a brick.
But of this kind God makes up pearls,
And such was she of the long blond curls.

Jigs

Good fortune smiled and brought us a friend,
For filling our need he was a godsend.
Condemned by the town as mad dog biter
With earned reputation as mean and a fighter.
The townspeople said that dog had to leave,
His banishment from town his only reprieve.
Per his master's request he came to our farm
Away from the town to cause no more harm.

When Jigs arrived it was love at first sight;
He felt right at home to our family's delight.
Like lion in the song who was born to be free
Not a thing on our farm to cause him to flee.
Sensing our pleasure and that we were agog
About his coming to live and be our dog,
His acceptance of us was true from the start,
To members of family he gave all his heart.

As companion and friend he treated us royal,
To guard and protect he remained ever loyal.
When mad bull threatened he knew he was needed,
And hearing one's call he instantly heeded.
When a salesman threatened Mom at the door
He retreated on high when Jigs came to fore.
Being handsome of visage he made us proud;
We'd boast of his exploits in words clear and loud.

There was no other dog with his strength and speed,
When the pack raced for rabbit Jigs took the lead.
Fearless he was when he tackled that skunk;
To kill that foul varmint took lots of spunk.
His biggest joy was the baby brother,
Excitement ran high when they played with each other.
There were gophers to catch and prairie explore;
Each day held for them new adventure in store.

Sad was the day our friend left us forever,
Fond memory of Jigs, cold death couldn't sever.
Forever a legend in our hearts he will be;
He left bondage of town for farm to be free.
Fate brought us together and did a good deed;
We were meant for each other in each time of need.
Time can't erase and thoughts of Jigs won't end,
For good memories of him our thanks does ascend.

Thankful

The hard times of life sometimes are best;
That they cause struggle and put one to test.
To look back and remember that one may say,
"Because of hard times I'm more thankful today."

How poignant are memories of bygone days
When hopes and prayers were people's mainstays.
'Twas time of homesteads, depression, and wars
When deprivation was theirs as inheritors.

Think of the homesteader proving his land
Building one-room shack the harsh winter to stand,
Then undisturbed sod of millenniums to plow
With beasts of burden and his sweat of brow.

Didn't have plumbing nor electric light for shack.
Mother Nature's call was to outhouse in back.
It was oil for the lamp and coal from shed,
And no water from tap but from well instead.

Saturday night's ritual was bath in a tub;
Clothes rubbed on a board with a rub-a-dub-dub.
Winter's clothes on line frozen stiff as a rope,
Relief of such drudgery not more than a hope.

No school bus at gate, it was walk to the school;
Eight grades in one room with one teacher to rule.
A pot-bellied stove with kids gathered round,
Hoping warmth to offset winter's cold could be found.

First wagon and horse then the Model-T Ford,
What was needful for life could barely afford;
Then stock market crash and the Great Depression,
How tough life could get was eye-opening lesson.

The greatest dilemma was food for table
For members of family and dwellers of stable;
Perhaps produce from garden and milk from cow,
Eggs and chicken, and lean bacon from sow.

Modern amenities of life didn't exist,
Being strangers to them weren't really missed,
But can you imagine such incredible toy
As Atwater-Kent radio to be theirs to enjoy.

No money for shows nor summer vacation,
A mood of despair hung over the nation;
But mothers and fathers who cared for their own
Kept kids afloat until they were grown.

Then came the great war for which they did serve,
The Pearl Harbor attack would test heart and nerve.
At Uncle Sam's urgent call all rallied as one,
And suffered the call until victory was won.

Having lived in two worlds one can't help compare
The limousines of today with old gray mare,
And smelly old lamp with electric light to illumine,
Which so handy to switch all will determine.

The outhouse in back one will never forget
How one scraped off snow before bottom was set.
For convenience top prize indoor plumbing for house,
How wondrous the comfort for sibling and spouse.

When the washer and dryer made their debut,
How colossal the drudgery they did subdue.
You just push buttons and they leap to respond,
It's so fairy tale-like waving a wand.

How convenient the thermostat to regulate heat,
Incessant lugging of coal now obsolete.
The time for cleaning does the vacuum abridge;
When you want a cool drink you go to the fridge.

Then the supermarkets what marvelous stores,
They'd be hard to believe by our ancestors,
As would the recliners who are watching TV,
Viewing the world come to their house to see.

What more could one ask then our age to enjoy
With the modern inventions for us to employ.
The hard times a dim dream of what used to be,
One's thankfulness now stems from past history.

Big Surprise

They thought it amusing what the young man said,
He was surprised that his dad now so wise,
For when growing up he thought him a dumbhead
When he chided and would to him sermonize.

As a teen he growled that Dad was a killjoy,
Never granted enough leeway to move,
He'd set galling limits his pride to annoy,
Forever stymieing his manhood to prove.

That you're young only once he paid no heed,
Would ignore that he too was once young.
To spoil any fun he was sure was Dad's creed,
The young man had a sharpness of tongue.

Persistent to push responsibility button,
To do the homework and earn a good grade;
Learn how to work and for play don't be glutton,
For falling short Dad was sure to upbraid.

When under Dad's roof he pushed his own thing,
Would use ruse to foil rule and set regimen,
When naysayed his way sharp arrows he'd fling,
By his scowl would hurl daggers again.

Poor Dad he regretted had borne his sharp sting,
Paternal charge enjoined to him did forget.
You don't understand, he brayed as an offspring.
Naught but freedom would his stiff neck unset.

When out of the nest and he now more wise,
He was amazed that his dad was true friend.
That Dad was so wise was for him big surprise,
A debt of thanks he now owed to amend.

Brothers

In the whole realm of human relations
Many factors will enter equations.
Most precious of course is love of a mother,
But don't downsize a brother for brother.

It's been said that blood is thicker than water,
Applies to family for both son and daughter,
But for sons in family there is special bond;
Compared to others kinship goes on beyond.

I guess it's because they do what they do,
They're so boisterous and they play to subdue.
From the time of cradle life is an adventure
As they ramble from venture to venture.

Just watch the boys before time for girls,
Perpetual motion either jumping or whirls,
One moment down to wrestle and struggle,
Then upright for some object to juggle.

Not a care in the world at this stage of life,
Unaware that up ahead, world of strife,
But this is the time when relations do weld,
And love for brother will ever be held.

It's a wonderful thing such feel for brother,
To share with him what you won't with another;
To walk down the years and cherish this bond,
No other kinship can to that correspond.

Pete

As I think back to then, I can see him now,
For he will ever be etched on my mind.
Not one to idolize nor to whom you'd kowtow,
But as a teacher he left others behind.

A tall bony redhead with a face like a horse,
His scrimpy hair parted off to the side,
A distant descendant from an immigrant Norse,
Over students he knew how to preside.

When assuming his most normal teaching stance
He'd forth and back rock from heels to his toes.
Then with serious demeanor and stern countenance,
He'd teach algebra's equations and ratios.

And teach them he would with chalk and the board,
Presenting problems and the how of solution,
Thus opening young minds for knowledge to hoard
By the process of day-by-day evolution.

A full-schedule teacher, he gave it his all;
Within his scope all the science and the math,
Also coach of sports from track to the ball,
And taxidermy a choice class on his path.

For the best of teachers Pete comes to mind,
For he wouldn't put up with tom-foolery.
It wasn't his fault if you left behind,
When you questioned he'd answer your query.

When all of his students think back to school,
They speak fondly of the great teacher Pete.
He was in charge and like a stubborn old mule
He forced knowledge on student and athlete.

Work

Life without work would be useless
Like clouds without water for rain.
One's sojourn here would be meaningless,
God's purpose for man then in vain.

When God in his wisdom gives gifts,
Talents to be availed of in toil,
The fruit from such union uplifts
And does judgment as useless despoil.

To earn keep as fruit of one's labor
Makes man happy and gives self-esteem.
He can look in the eye of his neighbor,
Have no need for respect to redeem.

When God created man in his image,
He as maker, bestowed blessing of toil
To fill the days of his pilgrimage;
It was his way for child not to spoil.

There is no greater role for a man
Than to toil and produce benefaction.
This fulfills his role as custodian
For which there's blessing and satisfaction.

For works will be judged in hereafter,
When one's record will be scrutinized there.
All work passing test will bring laughter,
But how sad if one's cupboard is bare.

Hope

Hope springs eternal in the human breast.
It's like yeast in the soul of a man,
That helps him rise up to meet each new test;
To think boldly that "I can, yes, I can."

It's like grist for the mill or fuel for the fire,
It gives courage to take up the strife,
For lofty ideals one cannot aspire
E'er hope emboldens and motivates life.

It's the mainspring of man that lifts up the dream:
That there's a future just waiting for him,
That hard work and success will bring self-esteem,
And pleasant life that is filled to the brim.

But if one can't escape a rain of hard blows,
And discouragement takes hold to afflict,
It's hope that will rescue and vanquish the woes,
To give courage to resume the conflict.

When finally one's years have run the course
And one's dreams yet remain unfulfilled,
In eternal life is yet hope to offer recourse,
With eons of ages in which to rebuild.

With eternal life in the offing, wide is your scope
For opportunity your dreams to complete.
With faith in Jehovah to undergird hope,
It is impossible to suffer defeat.

Roads

Have you ever been intrigued by a road
So that you wondered whereto it would lead?
Did curiosity win and prod as a goad
To take that road then your wont to accede?

As you set out on that unknown way
With high spirit and keen expectation,
Did detours and crossroads lead you astray,
And get you lost to your sad consternation?

The whole world is laced with such roads
That all beckon to take you somewhere,
To myriads of places and human abodes,
Just waiting for the devil-may-care.

But the wise ones will chart out a course
That will lead to their planned destination,
Knowing lostness will be font of remorse,
They take care on their earthly migration.

The road of life does too impel choices
With all those callings and isms to follow,
For each have hawkers with beckoning voices,
Confused pilgrims will be swayed to and fro.

Just a few will travel the high ground,
But the many take broad ways below,
Some go around like a merry-go-round,
Unwary travelers just follow the flow.

It is written to look for the straight gate
Where you may enter the road that is narrow.
If once on this road do not hesitate,
It'll lead you true and straight as an arrow.

Homes

At the very heart of the Creator's plan
Are homes to live in for created man,
That from birth to death into great beyond,
He need not be homeless as a vagabond.

When Adam and Eve were created as one,
A home in the garden for them was begun.
There, little ones learned at parent's knee
Sacred lore passed down from ancestry.

So restful and comforting is the home
When one has wearied of the world to roam;
How precious such refuge from eyes that can see
One's unmade face or other laxity.

No need for pretense in one's hiding place,
No fault or failure will cause disgrace.
One may let one's hair down so to speak,
A shelter from the cruel world for the meek.

The church home too the Redeemer's vision
As He bade disciples the great commission.
A place to gather for sheep of his flock
Where worship of God will their love interlock.

Divine is the vision of families together,
Each from their homes with church as a tether,
Friendships and kinships bonded here evermore,
For families of God to enjoy and explore.

'Tis forestaste of heaven the new Jerusalem,
Where homeward bound receive their diadem.
It's heavenly home of the bride and THE LAMB
Who will dwell forever with the great I AM.

A Friend

When steadfast and true can be said of a friend,
Prayers of thanks for that should ascend.
To have such a treasure is finer than gold.
Yes, it's finer, yeah! A thousandfold.

For talents of gold can't compare with a friend
Who offers friendship on which to depend.
In seasons of want or just to abide
When you need someone close by your side.

For deep in the heart is the yearning to share
And to know there is someone to care,
For pleasures and triumphs that gladden the heart,
Or all the bad things that tear you apart.

For greater are pleasures graced by good will
Of the friend whom your joy wants to fill.
It, too, lessens the pain and uplifts the mood.
The goodwill is like a heavenly food.

'Tis a pauper indeed who counts naught a friend;
No sadder words could ever be penned.
If such be one's lot, do another befriend;
Perhaps the deed then your plight will amend.

Freedom

If one were deprived, either beast or mortal,
Loss of freedom would be hardest to bear.
The words "liberty or death" forever immortal,
Freedom lost would cause the greatest despair.

Just cage up a tiger and what have you got?
A snarling beast glaring out in great rage.
The freedom once known it has not forgot,
Ever prowling to find a way out of cage.

What sorer loss but to take away freedom,
Impose punishment to deprive one of same.
More than all else inspireth the martyrdom,
The great sacrifice to one's freedom reclaim.

In this our day as in the days of ago,
We also have met the call to stay free.
That freedom we have, our children may know,
A beneficent gift form the deity.

If each age obliged this right to defend,
Dare this freedom we presumptuous receive?
For tyranny's grasp we must apprehend
Because it lurks, and ever seeks to aggrieve.

So count all your blessings in freedom's light,
To be a citizen in a land that is free;
For the difference as great as daylight to night
For those abiding in dark tyranny.

Struggle

When Adam and Eve by serpent beguiled
And their innocence and virtue defiled,
Disobedience's price was paradise lost
As their maker sought them out to accost.

No bread to eat but by sweat of the brow,
For in judgment this was God's solemn vow;
Struggle thy lot and banned from the garden
As His stance toward His creatures did harden.

Though paradise lost man given reprieve,
Sweat and toil now the way to achieve.
Bread for table daily challenge for all,
To comfort hunger and cruel famine forestall.

Now for mortals to be best they can be,
Will take struggle, fallen man's destiny;
For goals to be set though near or afar,
They must toil to many barriers unbar.

So what of decree that struggle we must,
Is the punishment to be the main thrust,
Or is there in it higher purpose for man,
To be more faithful than when he began?

Is not struggle a touchstone of character,
To gain endurance the greater factor?
When paradise regained, man thankful will be,
Of disobedience now knoweth reality.

Awe

How barren the soul that feeleth no awe
In a world displaying such splendor.
Pity the one who suffereth such flaw,
Not perceiving the hand of the render.

Oh, look in the mirror, thou blinded one,
Form a smile with your lips and your eyes,
Awe-filled you should be; what the creator has done.
He gave you eyes for to see your smile rise.

Consider a seed, perhaps small grain of wheat,
How it germinates and sends up a blade,
Then stretches toward sun to soak in the heat;
It's amazing how the kernels are made.

How truly astounding the salmon migration,
Without compass they traverse the sea
To reach place of birth to ensure procreation,
And for struggle death decreed destiny.

When He sends forth the storm in fury and sound,
Cracking lightning sets the sky all aglow.
At flash of the light peals of thunder resound,
And men and creatures seek for shelter below.

Have you sat on a bank, the moon shining above,
Its beams shimmering on the face of the water?
It entrances one's soul as will light-o-love,
The scene formed by the heavenly potter.

To feel no awe is to insult the creator,
His handiwork everywhere to be seen;
To laud His creation, there is nothing greater,
The Maker pleased with such discernment that keen.

Worth His Salt

Show me a man with pride in his work
And I'll show you a man worth his salt,
For he'll be a man who labor won't shirk,
No lesser words than "well done" will exalt.

How sorry the state of one who won't care,
Esteemeth not to be best he can be,
Seeks no high standard as goal to declare,
For shoddy work his tune fiddle-de-dee.

The job worth doing is worth doing well,
To do less will dishonor the workman.
Pride is the engine drives one to excel,
The motivator to do the best that he can.

What finer legacy than works well done?
They are monuments to the worth of a soul.
In the march of time they'll memory outrun,
For posterity will record on the scroll.

In time of demise the headstone should say,
"Worth his salt," if any questioner should ask,
Full measure of labor for each day's pay
As departed gave his best to the task.

Good News

When under a cloud most people yearn
For good news of the sun to shine through.
It's not very pleasant for one to sojourn
Without sun, for it'll good cheer subdue.

If a cloud of worry hangs over one's head,
Some crisis for harm seems impending.
If news should come to take away dread,
The good news makes for happy ending.

When calamity threatens and outcome's in doubt,
And wild rumors increase trepidation;
When the news comes to put them to rout,
It gives cause for great celebration.

Many are daunted by news of the day,
There but tidbits of hope to uplift,
but when news is good, it will gloom allay,
To the cast-down, a most welcome shift.

"How beautiful the feet that bring good news,"
The apostle said of those who are sent;
To those without hope their message renews
Hope of heaven for those who are penitent.

Be a man of good will and look for the best
To present as good news to the world.
Do that, my friend, and you will be blest,
For the feet will on you be impearled.

Vision

To perish or fail for lack of vision,
A fearful price to pay for such folly.
The height of folly was son of perdition;
To the drifter floweth much melancholy.

Big are the dreams that will reach for a star
As are those of the age of innocence,
But not counting the cost to aspire that far,
They are pipe dreams that lack any sense.

Many a person lives just for the moment,
Lacking vision of a right road to tread.
They idle their days, not seeking bestowment,
Of needed skills that would move them ahead.

To sacrifice virtue for stolen pleasure,
Such defilement brings to one tragic loss.
How lacking in vision to forfeit treasure,
To lose paradise unless cleansed by the cross.

As stewards of treasure some are so blind,
They build barns but don't store in heaven.
What's not sent ahead will be all left behind,
For heavenly dough it's no longer a leaven.

The worldly man who strives for success
With no thought for the fate of his soul,
Such lack of vision will leave him homeless,
At judgment, when they call heaven's roll.

This Too Will Pass

Life is famous for its ups and downs,
They come and go like the tide in the ocean.
The ups bring smiles, the downs bring frowns,
The change in mood plays tag with emotion.

So wherever the pendulum may swing at the moment,
One in high spirit or voicing alas,
There's one fact of life that's self-evident:
It's the saying "this too will pass."

Remembering your childhood, either lad or lass,
So many days had their moments of truth.
They all seemed so troubling, but then they'd pass.
They were gold in the lessons of youth.

So impatient are youth the teens to pass through,
To escape from unwanted control;
But waiting the years, their wish will come true,
Then in adulthood they will have to enroll.

When a vexing problem causes worry and fret,
The mind churning as in a morass,
When the solution does come, the fear will abet,
Then relief that the torment will pass.

In seasons of gladness when up on high ground
When all seems right in the realm,
Best savor the moments while such can be found,
E'er the valley takes over the helm.

When down on one's luck and run out of gas,
And one wonders what's the use of it all,
Remember valleys and peaks: this valley will pass,
The peak again will beckon and call.

As time marches on and one at an impasse,
If regret that one's dreams aren't achieved,
Don't let your hope dim, for this life will pass;
God restores all in Him who've believed.

Ill-Gotten Gain

To every human will come temptation,
The moment furnished by the tempter of men
For dishonest gain by one's perpetration,
If one discerns it beyond other's ken.

Perhaps phoney scale to shortfall a buyer
Who trusts you to afford a full measure.
He does not realize that you, the supplier,
Is pilfering a part of his treasure.

Haven't you heard one boast of his prowess
As a horse trader wheeler-dealer.
"I deflated his goods to make them seem less,
I beat him down," loudly crows the revealer.

Seizing the moment the looters run wild,
The mob feeding their passion and greed.
Grabbing unguarded spoil as a wanton child,
They rush pell-mell in the barbarous stampede.

When the income tax dents hard-earned receipts,
Perhaps resentment burns deep in one's heart.
How tempting to alter the balance sheets
To lessen income to hold back a part.

When needed tools are by company supplied
And they're stored for one's easy access,
Because others do, do you feel justified,
Taking stuff from that store to possess?

When the cashier takes your ten-dollar bill
As a payment for your purchase of gas,
When ringing the sale to give change from till,
If too much, will you allow it to pass?

Bank-robbing, shoplifting, insider trading,
They're all enticements for ill-gotten gain;
From cattle rustling to white-collar grafting,
Each the integrity of soul will profane.

When temptation arises, as surely it will,
Will you yield and your deed then ensconce?
If tempter wins out, voice of conscience you kill,
Veracity victim of your yielded response.

With tempter victorious and act carried out,
There'll be foreboding for having gone astray.
To thine own self be true no longer redoubt
The deed in limbo until the judgment day.

But know this fact, which is certainly true,
There's nothing hid that won't be made known.
The Scriptures reveal what the judger will do,
He'll bare your sin at the judgment throne.

Hammers

With the metal red hot and gripped with a tong,
The blacksmith hammers blow upon blow,
To the tune of the anvil like a brisk battle song,
He molds the metal before it loses its glow.

Be it humble abode or a country estate,
It takes hammer in hand to erect.
Putting pieces in place, one can then fabricate
According to blue-print of the architect.

When a pianist plays, fingers pressing the keys,
The sound of music wafts through the air.
The tune emanates from notes that he frees
When the hammers strike strings true and square.

Be one artisan, craftsman, or performing musician,
A useful tool in the hand of the sure
Is the hammer for pounding; it's his ammunition,
When creating so his dream will endure.

Life like a hammer rains many a blow
During the course of a human pilgrimage;
But as clay in God's hands, He doth foreknow,
How to mold His eternal heritage.

Giver or Taker

In the game of life the cards that are dealt,
Are played differently by givers and takers.
Givers are generous with spirit heartfelt,
Whereas takers reach for all on God's acres.

The testing begins from moment of birth
In the laboratory of experience called life.
They either grab for the last penny-worth,
Or they give to lighten loads in the strife.

As is often apparent when it's either/or,
The difference stands in stark relief.
The giver by nature is a contributor,
But for taker love of getting is chief.

Sweeter than honey is essence of givers,
Their generosity spreads balm in the land.
With joy in giving they are the free-livers,
They're thankful for opportunities at hand.

Their eye ever open to want of another,
These goodly folks respond quickly to needs.
With care and compassion as keeper of brother,
They perform gladly their beneficent deeds.

Whether giving of wealth or lending of hand,
Or gift of self to fill need as a friend,
Or loan of their talent or craft in demand,
Or giving credit or praise to commend,

Whatever the gifts they cause thanks to fly
And sweet odors to reach tester up there;
Thus thanks of the aided does God glorify,
For the giving does his love then declare.

Life Line

My friend asked the question, "Did you ask to be born?"
I surmised, "In all honesty, no."
Then he said, "Don't you think that's a matter to mourn?"
I replied, "Offhand, I don't know."

"Life's no bed of roses," he ventured to state.
"When they brought you forth, they did you no favor.
Cruel blows and hard knocks a most certain fate,
Aren't things you would normally savor."

"How so," I inquired, "can life be that bad,
That you'd state such a negative feeling?
There must be light in the tunnel and joy to be had
That would make it seem more appealing."

"No so," he declared, "if you'd give it some thought;
Just take stock of the world and the nation:
Murder and rape and society fraught
With the threat of nuclear annihilation.

"If that weren't enough, millions, suffering bad health,
The earth soiled with mindless pollution.
Now comes the plague AIDS, crept upon us with stealth,
Defying all attempts for solution.

"Furthermore, how depressing, the news is all bad,
As you listen to the events of the day.
Not one word of good cheer to make people glad,
The public wants that, the news people say.

"As to friendship," he asked, "can a true friend be found,
Who'll respect you and love you forever?
There's no one like that, though you search the world round,
Who wouldn't your friendship dissever.

"So, see what I mean when I suffer the thought,
It would be better to have never been born.
If that's all there is, this life battle fought
With no victory, no reward, but a thorn."

"Such lament," I declared, "ne'er before did I hear,
Of pessimistic and low-down feeling.
To uplift you, my friend, it's abundantly clear,
Will require strong cure for your healing.

"I grant you, my friend, that like a river your life
Is fraught with whirlpools, rapids, and shoal.
But don't for the struggle lose heart for the strife,
For there is sure hope for your soul.

"So take comfort, my friend, don't ever despair;
From despair there is one to deliver.
To a city of gold and a land sweet and fair;
It's on the other side of the river."

"But the river," he cried, "I'm unable to cross.
It has hazards and whirlpools galore."
To that I replied, "A bridge shaped like a cross
Spans that river from shore to shore."

"But herein lies a simile: that bridge is a man.
He came down from the heaven above.
At the Father's request and according to plan,
He became the bridge by an act of his love.

"But to make him your bridge, it's required of you
To bow down and accept him as Lord.
Then a lifeline He'll throw with aim that is true.
Grab hold by faith, and He'll pull you on board."

Reflection

Having lived my life I look back and reflect:
Were I to start my life over tomorrow.
Searching my memory to enhance retrospect,
What apt lessons from the past would I follow?

So starting anew using wisdom in store,
I'd tame exuberance to sow the wild oats.
Some pleasures of youth cause rue evermore,
Do bring ills for which there aren't antidotes.

I'd heed the axiom that age begets wisdom,
That school of life has earned graybeards degrees.
With their experience, they would speak with aplomb;
To be your mentors, they would glad be devotees.

I'd be keenly aware life quickly flies by,
To waste time would be the height of folly.
That this is one truth that the aged descry,
More than else, this causes them melancholy.

As life heaven's gift, I'd savor each moment,
With my family would live each day as last.
I'd gorge on ripe fruit, the creator's bestowment,
For sport of day, be an avid enthusiast.

I'd set my sights early on goals for my life,
So there'd be a good harvest at reckoning;
To make all worthwhile the struggle and strife
On the day the grim reaper comes beckoning.

I'd be more alert to the marvels of nature,
To the dewdrop clinging fast in the morning.
To enjoy snowy mountains of God's portraiture,
And the wildflowers in the meadows adorning.

Above all else to heed light that's been shed:
Love God first, but also love ye the brother.
In the last analysis, it can safe be foresaid,
There'll be judgment how you treated the other.

So from the reflection at life's eventide,
Would I really all those lessons hold fast?
'Tis only conjecture how the lessons would guide.
I can't prove it with a life that is past.

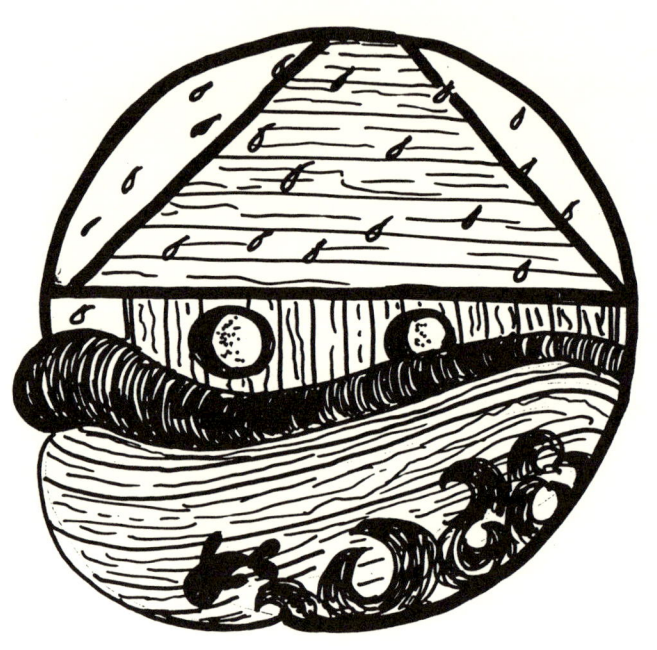

Safe Passage

How strange the spectacle of human existence
Begun in the cradle of a mother's womb.
Born to earth with loud cries of resistance,
To engage in struggle till returned to the tomb.

So birth then the genesis of the human soul,
From whence life on earth is given its start.
Thus begins the great drama to seek common goal,
Of happiness, joy, and contentment of heart.

Time is of essence per the creator's design,
The amount allotted each soul a precious gift.
Time of life must be lived, one cannot resign;
E'er to do so would be to set soul adrift.

Each life to be lived is like a ship on the ocean,
But its launch is on the great sea of life.
As each sets sail and stirs into motion,
Unknown dangers for shipwreck are rife.

Without chart and compass, and a pilot to steer,
Even seaworthy ships run aground.
May the question be asked, can a soul run clear,
Without pilot to that port where it's bound?

There is such a one, but He pilots an ark
That carries souls on that perilous sea.
All that's required is for one to embark;
For safe passage He's life's guarantee.

The Hand

When God created the heavens and earth
And formed man from the dust of the ground,
He breathed life into man at the moment of birth
To have dominion o'er the whole world around.

To each one a body, many parts to the whole,
All are subject to control of the mind.
Human nature imbued with spirit and soul,
Such a medley where else can you find?

All are essential for good of the whole,
God arranged them in pure symmetry.
The parts are assigned to perform a role,
Such conception a profound mystery.

Each is important not one o'er the rest,
Their many functions so diverse and grand,
But of family of parts God did his best
When He designed the incredible hand.

Just consider the hand at behest of a man
Performs with skill and intricate control.
It quickly responds to carry out plan
And does marvelously fulfill its role.

For grasping, twisting, or any maneuver
The mind signals the hand to comply,
Which leaps to respond as obedient mover
To immediately master's wish satisfy.

For example, a flag passing by in review,
Which you honor with salute of the hand,
Each time you do that you signal anew,
Love of country for which it does stand.

Is this not a marvel to move one to awe,
God's multiciplicity of design at command?
Of the billions of hands the creator foresaw,
He designed no other with prints like your kind.

Gloria Dei

How majestic a church with a steeple on top!
Like a finger pointing up, is its spire.
'Tis signpost from God saying, "Here you should stop,
There's a blessing for your soul to acquire."

How exalted the church, which at top of its spire,
Has the symbol of that one suffering loss,
Who took on himself your blame and hell-fire:
This symbol at very top is the cross.

How beneficent the Christ this way to remind
Straying children the way up is through Him,
And by pointing His way to lost humankind,
They'll know way to reach home of the seraphim.

How blessed is the land with many a steeple,
It tells the world men of faith there do dwell;
That there in that place God has a people,
And hasn't abandoned it to the infidel.

There's a beautiful church perched on a hill
With its spire pointing up toward the heaven.
Just the sight of the church gives one a thrill,
For all around it spreads heavenly leaven.

When building the church, it was named Gloria Dei,
So insightful were those folks from the past.
Guided were they, when they took time to pray,
And its meaning, "Glory to God," held them fast.

Childhood Fantasies

Childhood is the time to fantasize,
To build castles in the sky.
'Tis normal for youth to rapturize,
To spread wings and soar on high.
When fantasies take off and fly,
They arouse desires playing possum;
Then the hidden will rise and identify,
That reality may bud and blossom.

Fantasies then mature to dreams,
And dreams to ultimate fruition,
Which decides path dreamer deems,
Best fulfills the earthly ambition.
'Tis pivotal the role of childhood
With its fantasy and imagination.
It inspires and makes understood,
Adulthood goals for actualization.

Understanding

One day as I sat and mused
And got serious in my mind;
I thought of three imponderables
Dwarfing all of humankind.
Struggling with these I deduced
They were in the realm of sublime,
That nothing a mortal enables;
Understanding God and space and time.
With the universe providing space
Without limit, so they say,
How can beings that area embrace,
Can even eternity such vastness outstay?
But above all the space and time,
God, omnipresent, omniscient, immortal.
When with Him in the aftertime,
We'll understand when changed from mortal.

One's Dream

Some people seem to be born with a dream,
Have no question as to road they will tread,
As if from birth they are following a beam,
From the cradle by its rays they are led.
With goal set before they formulate plan,
They're that sure of this dream in their heart,
They'll be politician or perhaps artisan,
Their inclination has gripped firm from the start.

Then there are those never know what they want,
Though they yearn, no dream captures their heart,
Their mind without vision and this does them haunt,
They're rudderless and a course cannot chart.
Can't create ripples but just float with the tide,
Will follow path of the least resistance;
With no goal to achieve they simply abide,
Their whole future to be determined by chance.

But I knew of a man, a poor lost soul,
Who was wandering from pillar to post,
Just so it paid though it be without goal,
He'd take whatever though it be hindermost.
But fate took a hand, perhaps mother's prayer
To mighty mover and shaker above,
For that luckless soul were brought forces to bear,
He found his dream, though here and there took a shove.

Wondering

Who hasn't looked up in the dark of night,
Perhaps the moon shining bright in the sky?
As you peer at the stars of the lesser light,
You wonder how did God make them and why.

But more than the how and why in your wonder
Is the riddle of the inscrutable who:
Was the beginning of God in fire and thunder,
Or was "I AM" beyond the point thitherto?

What is the glue that binds all together,
The mighty force that holds feet to the ground?
You wonder how gravity works as a tether,
Why spin of earth doesn't hurl you outbound.

Then there's the riddle of chicken and egg,
'Tis conjectural which first did appear.
For the agnostics, proven answer they beg,
But for believers creation's answer is clear.

Isn't it strange differing psyches in men;
Why two people so disparate in creed?
For one the true God meaneth all in his ken,
But the other will pay his birthright no heed.

Haven't you wondered about the wisdom tooth,
This strange molar that is a late riser?
A useless adjunct may be nearer the truth
Than the myth that it maketh one wiser.

But greatest wonder is God's love for man;
Why mighty God wants wee man as his friend,
And had such compassion He set up the plan
To take him home and give life without end.

So liven your spirit and stay tuned to life;
Be ye sensate, not wooden and blundering.
In this wide world there are mysteries so rife
They cannot help but rouse you to wondering.

Abandoned

As you travel along o'er the lone prairie,
Your eyes searching for something to see,
As you cover the miles, now and then will appear
An abandoned homesite of a pioneer.

With tumbled-down buildings weathered by sun
That are well on their way to oblivion,
Perhaps creaky old windmill perched on a tower,
The pump broken down, the wind worthless for power.

As you peer at the scene telltale signs you can see,
Accumulations from toil now junk and debris.
Strange farming machines from a bygone day
Now abandoned to nature to rust and decay.

Fenceposts with wire once stretched to enclose
Treasured acres of land long bid adios,
Now broken and scattered will no longer hold:
It tells a sad story for all to behold.

As you take in the scene you muse and ponder:
You wonder from whence that pilgrim did wander
To pick out this spot from all the wide earth,
Where his sweat and toil could create place of worth.

What were his dreams and what time did he come
To join the ranks of the adventuresome?
Did he sail the wide ocean to reach a new shore,
Or was it westward-ho for new land to explore?

Through all the struggle was there ever reward,
Or satisfied feeling that he was a landlord?
Did the home ever ring with laughter and mirth,
Or discouragement stifle and for gladness cause dearth?

It is a sad scene and a strange mystery,
What really happened at this abandonee.
Did the pilgrim move on to a better way?
The mystery perhaps sealed until the judgment day.

Lonely Cemetery

Skirting Saskatchewan up north on the prairie,
To the south within sight of the Bear's Paw,
Is home for departed, a lonely cemetery,
You walk therein with reverence and awe.

For here lie at rest both neighbor and friend,
Gathered here within reach of each other,
As if by their closeness it would ever portend,
Death had sealed them as sister and brother.

As you note the names of those early pioneers,
Most were cattlemen, merchant, or farmer,
As homesteading folks it made them all peers,
To survive, they had need for strong armor.

To bear many hardships was common to all,
Testing nerve and their will to endure,
To start with nothing as most did would appall
All the weaker prone to feel insecure.

For all these departed had a story to tell,
Their tomb monuments but relics of each.
Had stories been told before the death knell,
What great lessons for all they would teach.

For these were the ones who met the test
As they challenged this raw wilderness.
The fact they won as survival of fittest,
They'd surely speak with persuasiveness.

Methinks they would teach to be a good neighbor,
To have faith for stiffening endurance,
That cheer and optimism lacing hard labor
Would be ingredients for their perseverance.

Montana

When our forebears established the borders
To create the great states of our nation,
The land of one as set down by recorders,
Evokes from many a rare fascination.

What enchants is its wide-open spaces
With big sky and fresh air to breathe free.
It's all that room the Montanan embraces
Without hindering hoards of humanity.

From the Bitterroots to the far-off Dakotas
O'er towering mountains, foothills, and plain,
Hath not the creator exceeded his quotas,
When allotting to one such a varied terrain?

To the north edging up to the stratosphere
In traversing the highway to the sun,
One may view the home of the glacier,
Here trickling waters begin seaward run.

Then far south and Montana will take you
To the gates of unique Yellowstone.
Here cauldrons rumble and geyser spew—
Such phenomenon where else can be shown?

How vast is its eye-stretching prairie,
It expanse seemeth here to forever,
Here grassland creatures find sanctuary,
And there's room for a bold man's endeavor.

With much treasure this state has been blessed,
Laden with minerals, forests, and cattle.
With scenic lakes and broad rivers it's dressed;
For its honor loyal sons will do battle.

It's a land that offers rare freedom,
For those spirits who need room to roam.
To those of such ilk it speaks, "Come!
In Montana you will find your true home."

Basic Training

Uncle Sam bade him come; there was a war to be fought,
Protecting home was no longer his haven.
A young man fearful and sore distraught;
What came next on his mind ever graven.

"Fall in line," roared the sergeant, "and stand at attention,
From now on you're no longer your own.
Know I don't molly-coddle, lest misapprehension,
Makes you think I'm a mere chaperone.

"Don't ever forget this is war to the finish,
No quarter asked nor will any be given.
There's no room for the sissy nor the babyish.
To be fighters all of you will be driven.

"When I bark a command, you don't think, you react!
You will move out on the double.
Just mark it down well and take note of this fact:
You obey, or you'll get into trouble.

"We'll march you and drill you until you're foot sore.
In fierce combat the weak won't survive.
When you've reached outer limit, you reach down for more,
It's the strong with best hope to stay live.

"Basic training is tough; it's intended that way,
When you're through, you won't easily rattle.
With the training received you won't comrades betray:
A good account you will give in the battle.

"The end result of this training to which you're consigned
Is discipline, discipline, discipline.
For the duration you're in, to that be resigned,
Until our flag flies over Tokyo and Berlin."

Orientation

"We're just a cadre now," said the First Sergeant, "but we intend to build up until we reach the authorized number of 130 men and 4 officers. More recruits will be arriving until we come up to full strength. In the meantime we'll be functioning as a company and will pull duty assignments. Beginning immediately, you will check the bulletin board daily for assignments. For those of you pulling guard tonight for the first time, I'm here to orient you on what that duty entails.

"I just came over from the island to help form this new company. It was really a mess over there after the attack on Pearl. We were on full alert twenty-four hours a day. Not only were we expecting further attacks by the Japs, but saboteurs were everywhere. It was scary as hell. All sentries on guard carried live ammunition with orders to shoot anyone who failed to halt and identify themselves. There were several incidents of saboteurs sneaking up on guards and stabbing them in the back. I cannot overemphasize for you recruits how important it will be for you to keep on extreme alert. You will be issued live ammunition with orders to fire on anyone that fails to obey your order to halt.

"Those of you assigned guard tonight, report to the guard shack fifteen minutes early to pick up your firearm and ammunition. A guard officer will be making his rounds to check on you and will bring a replacement when your shift is up."

Driving slowly through the night, the guard officer came to a stop and shut off the motor. "This is the outer parameter of the base," he said, "and you will patrol along this fence down to the corner and back. Remember, no smoking on guard. I'll be back at 4:00 A.M. with your replacement." "Sir," I stammered, "it's pitch black. I can't see a thing." "You'll get used to the night," he replied. "Just follow back and forth like I told you." "Yes sir," I said as I saluted and muttered to myself, "I just hope I don't fall into a hole out here in the dark." The officer drove off quietly into the night.

Stepping softly, I started groping my way slowly up the fence line. *Man, this is dark,* I thought as I peered nervously about. Stopping abruptly and turning 360 degrees, I stared intently into the darkness but could see nothing but inky blackness. Reaching out I touched the fence line for reassurance.

Suddenly I heard a strange noise off to my right. Startled, I strained to see what it was. I could see nothing. Slipping the safety off, I swung the gun frantically to the right ready for instant action. *There has got to be something or someone sneaking around out there,* I thought, but told myself sternly not to panic and start shooting up the place. Standing deathly still for what seemed like an eternity, I strained my ears to pick up that sound again, but all I could hear was my heart pounding. Realizing that I couldn't stand frozen to this spot the rest of the night, I cautiously took a step, then another, and then moved slowly forward again. *Boy, at this rate,* I thought, *this is going to be a long night.*

Barely calmed down, I was suddenly startled by a dog barking furiously off to my left on the other side of the fence. The sound was magnified by the cool still air of the night. Really shook up, my heart pounding again, I wondered how much more of this I could stand. Again frozen to a spot and every nerve taut with fear, I listened intently trying to recognize what the dog was barking at. After what seemed like forever, I finally decided that the dumb hound must be barking at me. Summoning what courage I had left, I started moving forward again.

Moving slowly along the fence line, I gradually calmed down and started to feel a certain sense of satisfaction that I could survive this night after all. "You had better not get too cocky," I told myself, the first sergeant's scary tales about the Hawaiian Islands still lurking in my mind.

As I was thinking these thoughts, suddenly out of the night, a shout of command, "Halt." I could hear the click of a rifle being cocked. "Halt yourself," I thundered back as I cocked my gun ready to fire. Every nerve and muscle tensed, I strained to see my challenger, but couldn't see a thing. I wondered frantically, *What do I do now?* The suspense was almost unbearable, but then a hesitant voice queried out of the blackness, "Are you on guard too?" Grasping the situation immediately, I heaved a big sigh of relief and blurted, "Yes, I'm on guard. You sure scared the you know what out of me." "Hey, I'm sorry, pardner. I could hear you, but I couldn't see you," he said. He sighed. "It sure is comforting to run into someone out here in this dark who isn't going to stab you in the back." "Boy, you can say that again," I affirmed as we groped our way together to fortify one another and shoot some bull.

A Lesson

Ordering the corporal off to the side,
The sergeant in his most secret mode,
Cupped his mouth and leaned close to confide:
"I've volunteered you for an episode."

"We are to report to the Wing Commander
To be assigned to a most ticklish mission.
But understand this, he's only a bystander,
If we're apprehended on this expedition."

The Wing Commander, a cocky young blade,
Said, "At ease," as he returned the salutes,
Then laid out a plan for a wild episode
To be carried out by two gas squad recruits.

"That bunch of inspectors from Washington, D.C.,
They need a lesson they will never forget.
For one week to wear gas masks, they issued decree;
Decreed for other, but not for them, not well met.

"Their team is housed in an officers' barrack,
They share these quarters all by themselves.
The gist of the plan is to mount an attack,
Then disappear like two mischievous elves.

"The time of attack will be four this morning,
When you approach the two doors of their barrack,
Be stealthy as cougars to forestall forewarning,
We want these guys to be each in his sack.

One will sneak inside and set tear gas grenade,
The other will lock the door on far side.
Then tearing outside you'll complete their stockade
By locking door; then let your feet be your guide."

"The action will start when you pull the pin,"
The Wing Commander had said in high glee.
At the loud noise of "pop," pandemonium set in,
They shouted, "Gas," as they leaped up to flee.

As the corporal and sergeant watched from afar,
They smashed windows and doors in their panic,
Each bursting outside like shooting star,
In BVDs their cold fury volcanic.

The base in an uproar, the police ordered to track
The perpetrators of this dastardly deed,
But the two gas recruits were hid in a shack,
Then dispatched off the base with high speed.

Sacred Ground

That shrunken coconut not much to look at
But for one it is a treasured memento,
For it brings to mind an island habitat
Where coconuts grow in a far archipelago.

The image of palm trees yet seems exotic;
To pluck a coconut all the men of one mind,
GIs climbing up trees seemed so chaotic,
Risking life so they could mail home a find.

The thunder of guns had barely subsided,
Debris of battle everywhere to be found.
With issue of winner by conflict decided,
The bold conquerors took possession of ground.

A great craze was on to find a souvenir,
A priceless trophy would be Japanese sword.
Their feel toward the enemy was so cavalier,
Only contempt toward the foe they'd accord.

One day a soldier strayed alone far afield,
Reconnoitering for whate'er could be found,
Crawling through jungle grizzly find it would yield;
A score of skeletons lay in jungle compound.

Inspecting the site the evidence seemed clear,
Enemy soldiers bivouacked here for the night.
Some weapon of war had sought them out here,
So with loved ones they could ne'er reunite.

First impulse of soldier was look for a sword,
But bad conscience then took over the man.
To pick among bones the thought he abhorred,
It seemed so savage like the act of barbarian.

For reflection set in and brought about sadness;
There came the feeling that this sacred ground,
For faraway loved ones would suffer the cruelness
Of not knowing if their loved ones were found.

Gambler's Dirge

He was just a bystander watching the game;
The winners and losers, he'd hear them exclaim.
The stakes were low but it did so excite,
When asked to sit in, he accepted invite.

He was new at poker but soon learned the way;
You must cover the bets to continue to play.
As he anted in pot for five-card draw,
All eyes focused on him like a camera.

As fate would have it, he neither won nor lost,
Not realizing then, later on the great cost.
For the noose had tightened to this man ensnare;
His psyche now tuned to a devil-may-care.

At first the excitement titillated his soul,
Not even a hint, he was losing control.
But didn't take long before losses did mount,
Of dwindling treasure, of this, did not count.

The fire in his soul was now to recoup;
That his luck would change, of hope was dupe.
The gambling fever had grabbed him firm in its grip;
Ever deeper in debt, this gambler would slip.

The demon of compulsion now laughed in glee,
Another victim in dungeon, chained in slavery.
Who imbibed for raw courage, but anted in vain,
For luck of the draw, better fate wouldn't deign.

Now nothing held back twin monsters to feed;
Where a buck could be garnered that source he'd bleed.
Alcohol to quench thirst and frenzy the urge
To ante the money for that sad gambler's dirge.

With hope doomed to Hades like prodigal with swine,
Things didn't turn around till power from divine,
Raised him out of the pit to life more sublime,
As he anted up for the very last time.

Long Night

She was sleek and white that grand luxury liner,
In tranquil times, voyagers bore to and fro,
But cause of victory did now reassign her
To task of transport of Uncle Sam's GI Joe.

"Time to doomp the garbage," the Dutch captain said,
He always broadcast at set of the sun,
Now as ghost in the night zigzagging ahead,
The *Pau-la-la* had strange action begun.

For word had been spread of a submarine scare,
Extreme precautions would be taken this night.
A mood of uneasiness swept through the air,
Spreading quickly as ship warned of its plight.

All crewmen to stations and troops to their bunks,
Complete blackout to be enforced above deck;
As orders rang out men staggering like drunks
On heaving ship to their hatches did trek.

Each now intent on instructions forthcoming,
No jesting now by the silly of heart,
For fear of unseen each soldier succumbing,
Of torpedoes that could tear ship apart.

They said, "Lay out your stuff for instant access,
Your life preserver and canteen of water.
Be aware of surroundings and how to egress,
To find a life boat keep an eye for the spotter."

Thus began that long night of anxious foreboding,
Imaginations running wild in the bunk,
Of perils in water the mind now exploding,
Should this troop ship by torpedoes be sunk.

The image of sharks, perhaps great white shark,
A threat to send one to Davy Jones's Locker,
Or could you be found in huge ocean so stark,
The alternative to the mind was a shocker.

No atheists in foxholes, soldiers do say,
So too, submarines draw men close to their maker,
For fervent was prayer to save from doomsday,
That the zigzags would from sub be the shaker.

At dawn's early light men noting ship's course,
The *Pau-la-la* westward straight from the sun
Brought sighs of relief and thanks with discourse,
That high throttle and zigzagging had won.

Forty

Birthdays may come and birthdays may go
But there's one many wish wouldn't show.
It's the fortieth one, which dismays and shocks,
For the fears of getting old it unlocks.

"Life begins at forty" is a saying that's true.
That only young enjoy life is all ballyhoo.
As the front forty was a school of hard knocks,
The thing that once did, no longer shocks.

With this experience good years should come
To better live life to the maximum.
Up ahead should be smooth, as you know the score,
And shouldn't make mistakes you did heretofore.

For o'er the horizon you'll soon lay down,
Burdens now furrowing your brow in a frown.
Like the bird of the field with emptied nest,
You too will have time for comfort and rest.

Those long-delayed dreams may now be revived;
Far-off places to see, time may have arrived;
Perhaps paint brush in hand to capture a scene,
Or hammock to know, or more knowledge to glean.

So cease to forebode, there's nothing to fear.
Give good expectation a chance to appear.
Embolden your courage, and expect the best.
A great future's before with which to be blest.

The Mall

The mall is a marvel of the modern age;
Here humans gather from country and town.
For many, the trip is daily pilgrimage;
Called the mall people, such is their renown.

A most remarkable structure, the shopping mall,
Providing comfort in the harshest of clime.
Though storming outside, inside snugness to all,
No matter what, it ever like summertime.

For the people watchers, what opportune place
To lounge in comfort and take in the sight.
With eager mind and keen eyes to keep pace,
They'll view humans in a most humorous light.

Conspicuous in mall are health nuts awalking,
They're strung out alongside walls periphery.
Serious this business, 'tis no time for talking,
They're counting minutes and rounds as their key.

As pedestrians go by, watchers covertly eye;
They note the bumps, every color, and shape.
There's diversification watchers cannot deny,
Some end products leave their mouths all agape.

There's short and tall, featuring fat to the lean;
Encumbered mothers screaming, "Junior, come here."
Or perhaps aged grandparents to dignify scene;
Every race is found in this atmosphere.

If there were any question, our land melting pot,
Every foreigner should make trek to our malls.
It then will be clear, what freedom has brought;
They'll see a spread like in great banquet halls.

The Hook

As the greatest invention since time began,
They say the wheel should rate the first look.
But have you considered the things that a man
Can perform with the use of a hook?

The concept is simple, just a curve at the end,
But consider all the things it can do,
Be it catch, be it pull, hold, or suspend,
With the hook one is armed to subdue.

For example, the trout feels secure in the brook
But the angler knows how to outwit it.
With lure of the bait and set of the hook,
He will catch it and make it submit.

When a boat rides at anchor, it won't go adrift,
For it can't float away with the tides.
As hook grips the bottom, the anchor won't lift,
And the boat on the waves safely rides.

Have you watched a climber ascending a cliff,
Grappler hooks gripping rock o'er his head?
Suspended below and the rope taut and stiff,
Up he goes safe and bold-spirited.

With canvas in place a rug maker sits,
With the hooks and his skill to combine.
Deftly hooking each loop, he, the yarn interknits,
Creates a rug with a lovely design.

For the billions of earth, what a mess there'd be,
Weren't there hooks from which to suspend,
For where would one hang one's dungaree?
To vanquish clutter, they are a godsend.

Crest

What's in a word may surprise you to know,
When you explore the full breadth of its meaning.
So let's choose a word and permit knowledge to grow
By deciphering and patiently gleaning.

A word comes to fore at my mind's eye behest
With meaning common but yet so profound,
Composed of five letters; you pronounce the word "Crest."
Now let us bandy its meaning around.

It's the crest on a rooster, which is called the comb,
It suggests kingly and regal port.
One cannot help sense those creatures' aplomb,
As they crow loudly and their fair ladies court.

Who hasn't been charmed by the arch of the neck,
And crest of mane like decor on medallion,
With nostrils flared and flashing eyes to bedeck
The noble form of a proud prancing stallion.

A brave soldier of war how else to adorn
But by a heraldic crest on his helmet,
To mark feats of arms for which he was born,
Which so gallantly, need of country, he met.

As one's eye wanders afield to the vistas beyond
To the north, to the south, east, or west,
Whether it's mountains you see or a nearby mound,
It's the top of the rise that's the crest.

Who hasn't been awed by huge waves on the ocean,
The surfer riding each wave from the crest?
Imposing the force that sets such in motion;
For exultant surfing, wild waves are the best.

When a river runs wild and floods o'er the land
And all things in its path put to test,
The danger won't yield, nor will hope be at hand
Until that river reaches its crest.

So if that be its meaning, "it's the top of its kind,"
Wouldn't it make sense to choose the best?
For tartar control and great flavor to find,
When selecting toothpaste, why don't you choose Crest?

Tanked Up

It all began when they met on the street.
They were so happy to see one another.
Extending their hands each other to greet,
Each greeted as though long-lost brother.

"Say, how have you been?" Hank said to Fred,
"I haven't seen you for a month of Sundays."
"Couldn't be better, you old arrowhead,"
Fred replied, but then joked, "It was Mondays."

"Hey, I'll buy you a beer," Fred said to Hank.
"Pardner, I can't beat an offer like that!"
"Let's go to Joe's and tap watering hole tank,
We'll hoist a few and catch up on some chat."

"What'll it be?" asked the friendly barmaid.
"Draw two," said the big spender Fred.
Then pulled out money for the beer to be paid,
From then on, there was a lot to be said.

"Say, I'm getting dry," Fred said to Hank.
"Draw two more," Hank said to the maid.
Having now lost track of each toast and clank,
No longer would they frank talk evade.

"Shay, Fred, you old——, ish your turn to buy."
"You don't shay!" "Yes, I shay," cackled Hank.
"If thash how you feel, I'm shaying good-bye,
You mush be drunk," Fred was perfectly frank.

Staggering outside, Fred climbed in his car.
He roared away in a spray of gravel.
And so it was, from good time in bar,
The judge said, "Guilty," and pounded his gavel.

Doing the Puyallup

There isn't much new at the fair
To be seen from year to year,
But there's something about the affair,
That rouses feelings in one that endear.

Perhaps it's that smell that allures,
Of hamburgers smothered in onions,
Tempting even the connoisseurs
To indulge while easing their bunions.

If a people watcher you are,
Where else can you find such a spread?
From country and town near and far,
Come the gentry to chucklehead.

Or perhaps the loud beat of music
Of Green River CC or the Shoppe,
Just watching the fans is a kick,
As they stomp and clappity-clop.

How truly American the fair,
Capitalism at work in the booth.
"Come close," says the hawker with flair,
"No better knife in the world; that's the truth."

Then as you view each exhibit
Such as painting, floral, or craft,
Note nothing will genius prohibit
When devotion drives handicraft.

But the heart of the fair is the shed,
All the barnyard residents there.
Cockle-doo crows the Rhode Island Red,
His blue ribbon, "I'm the best," doth declare.

For a dose of fun and good cheer,
You should add the fair to your cup,
For there'll be a hole in your year
If you fail to do the Puyallup.

The Billy Bum

He was really just a nothing chap,
But everybody's friend.
Even proud of mien he could entrap:
They'd for his hand contend.

He was known as the Billy Bum
Among people of the town,
But the aural air of the adventuresome
Had earned him some renown.

Of stature, just a wee man,
But a sort of tilt of his head
Would strike you like a dandy dan,
Though he didn't own a bed.

Though shiftless, slack, and lazy,
He'd disarm one with his grin.
How he fared was truly hazy,
For to him to work was sin.

Of wealth naught but a jaunty hat
And the clothes upon his back.
Where he hung his hat was his habitat,
Odds and ends filled up his pack.

Though he called this town his home,
It was only in summer's sun.
When the wild goose honked, it was time to roam,
Winter's odyssey was then begun.

Whereto this Billy wandered
Was a most mysterious thing.
Perhaps he followed the hummingbird
Where it had its winter's fling.

When winter's blast was over
And the snowbirds on the fly,
The town looked for this rover
To show up by and by.

For the town yet wrapped in doldrum
From winter's sore attack,
Needed magic of the Billy Bum
To get it back on track.

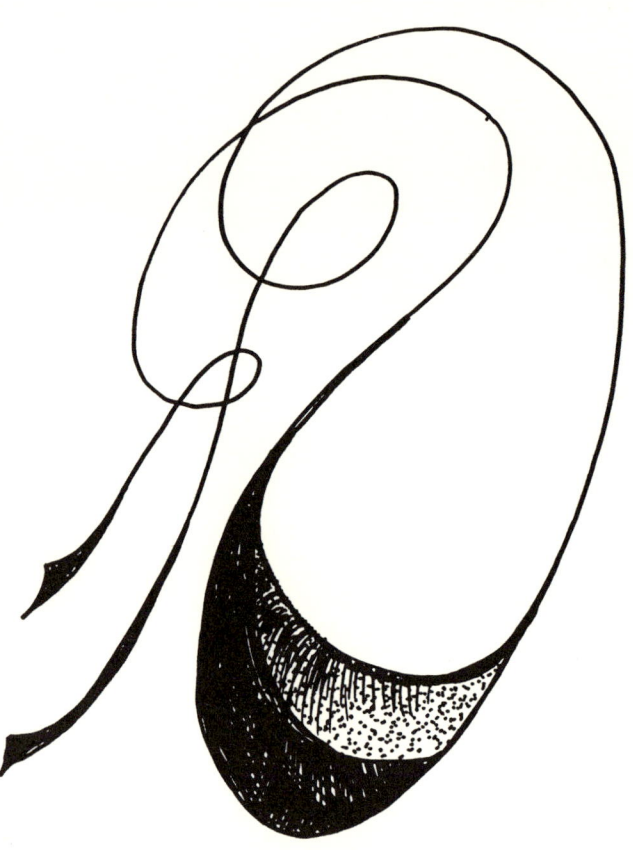

Slingflingers

What lad has not tested slingflinging skill
And been tempted by an off-limit target?
If target was hit, he claimed not of free will;
'Twas an accident, he'd say in regret.
One off-limit target enticing to hit
Tempted one to test slingflinging skill.
The eye of prize turkey seemed test to befit,
But after hit the feathered fowl did lie still.

Did not David the shepherd defeat the giant
Choosing five smooth stones from a brook?
When scoff of Goliath made David defiant,
He slung a stone and his measure he took.
For as weapon of choice did not David enshrine
The slingshot as a device of great skill?
With stone in web and violent whirl to combine,
He did his mission of great conquest fulfill.

You'd think the slingshot demanding such skill
Would arouse competing juice in the flingers;
Yet book of world records on this sport is nil
For rapid flinging who most stones are the slingers.
How many stones could a slingflinger fling
Should a slinger fling his stones in set time?
The fastest flinger would be slingflinging king;
To top pedestal that flinger would climb.

The Yahdies

Tom Foolery was at his mischievous best
When he whispered to Busy Body.
Seemingly serious but mostly in jest,
Stated, "Lutefish eaters are Yahdy."

Busy Body aquiver this news to tell,
Made beeline for Consummate Gossip.
Close to confide, almost touching lapel,
Said, "They're Yahdies," with a sarcastic quip.

"We must rush over to News Monger,"
They declared of this startling news.
"For us to delay and hold it longer,
We'd cheat the Yahdies out of their dues."

Eaves Dropper asked, "Who be the Yahdy?"
They all acted so sorely perplexed.
Mr. Meddler opined, "Your tale must be shoddy."
At accusation, they feigned being vexed.

Ms. Informer spoke, "Let's ask Paul Pry
To dig up the dope on the Yahdy.
To this enigma he'll find the why,
And the facts that the case does embody."

At meeting called by Herr Rumor Mill,
Paul Pry gave this startling report.
"The Yahdies are people who by free will,
Eat smelly fish with gusto in consort.

"This smelly fish they call Lutefish,
That's been treated with caustic lye.
That it has any taste is all gibberish,
But for Yahdies, it's their piece of pie."

"As to name Yahdy, it derives from word yah,
'Tis exclamation when impatient for fish;
But impatience soon turns to happy hurrah,
When cooked Lutefish comes ready to dish."

Learning the Hard Way

In the midst of the town was a country store,
The only trading post for miles around.
A naive young man became proprietor;
The lessons learned were for him most profound.

When a rancher or farmer came in to buy,
He'd say, "For now I haven't got wherewithal;
So, on my account do this purchase apply,
I'll pay the bill when I harvest this fall."

It caused trepidation when big farmer Frank
Would come a-stomping into the store.
When it came to snuff he was truly a crank,
If it stale, he would invective outpour.

Then he'd leave his order for young man to fill,
For Joe's tavern had irresistible call.
He'd say, "Don't have the money, so put on my bill,
I'll pay it up when I harvest this fall."

And so it was with country store patrons,
They looked for storekeeper to tide them over;
But, when in arrears, many ignored the duns,
They treated naive young man as pushover.

One day the young man took reality check:
The handwriting was getting plain on the wall.
He must take action to stave off a shipwreck,
For he couldn't pin down those harvests in fall.

"For paying your bill, which fall did you mean?"
The young man confronted Frank at the door.
"You pick a good fall," then what followed obscene,
Thus ended freefall at that country store.

Roses among Thorns

They say Machiavelli in his treatise, *The Prince,*
Deduced expediency above political morality.
In a practical sense it would be hard to convince,
Machiavellian does express the reality.

When the critical assayer depicts politicians
As being less than of pure reputation,
There's much better word to fit definition;
Self-aggrandizement will best describe allegation.

But let's set the stage for facts to be told,
First winning ballots, then fight to resist.
With prestige and power camped at the threshold,
Can winner's honor with such gods coexist?

Though motivation be sparked by purest intention,
The aspirant's claim, "I'm going to clean out the graft,"
Will he put to hard test, for he lacks comprehension
How power corrupts in this highest of craft.

For the chief drive of man is the lust for power,
To be dominant and impose his own will,
Though highest principles he shouts as avower,
It taketh iron for the ideals to fulfill.

It's the self with aggrandize that brings corruption
To increase power and one's wealth in portfolio,
Thus, self-aggrandizement causes ideals abruption;
Their words then are but bare braggadocio.

But let us be mindful of the good politician,
Here and there among thorns there's a rose;
Remaining true to your trust each deserves recognition,
In this loftiest of professions they chose.

Nomination of John Tower

In the halls of Congress great dramas unfold,
Fed by passion of players as they clash in debate,
With an eye to the nation, and partisan strategy so bold
To say they are right as they speak and orate.

Now comes a matter of great import,
The nomination for Secretary of Defense.
Will this be the time for some political sport?
The nation watches agog with suspense.

The Chairman of Armed Services is Mrs. Nunn's boy Sam,
They say he is truly a statesman.
He'll be fair and unbiased, there'll be no sham;
He'll do the best that he possibly can.

By reason of his win in the recent election,
Which the Democrats did deeply deplore,
Will this be the time in considering his selection
To weaken the president and even the score?

So what will be done with the nominee, John Tower,
With a reputation for women and drink?
The Democrats have the numbers, they have the power,
With nays prevailing, the nomination will sink.

With the battle now over, we know the results:
The nays carried against the boozer.
In post mortem, considering the barbs and insults,
The public must judge as to who was the loser.

The Mystic Right

They said it couldn't be done,
The odds set at five to one,
With pundits in doubt he could go the route,
They had him beat before he'd begun.

He said he had a mystic right,
But he kept it out of sight,
And the experts agreed that the fair-haired Swede
Didn't have it to make a fight.

The champ razor sharp for this hour,
His combinations a marvel of power,
As his muscles rippled they oohed and aahed
And felt sorry for Ingemar.

There was tension in the air
For those waiting for this affair,
As the small and the great came through the gate
Their impatience was hard to forebear.

Sharp rang the bell for round one;
Leaping forward as shot from a gun,
Both circled and pawed as crowd taunted and jawed;
They sparred for the prize to be won.

As he sat awaiting round three,
Urged to fight by the referee,
Ingemar glared at his foe; jumped up raring to go,
Determined no more should he flee.

Then it was that the mystic right,
Lashed out furiously with speed of light,
Landing full on the jaw with power awesome and raw,
What came next no one saw with foresight.

Seven times he got to his feet,
But to all they could see he was beat,
For though dead game, seven knock-downs became,
For the champ a most bitter defeat.

112

Moving swift to the center light,
The referee in command of the fight
Raised Ingemar's hand, a new champ in the land,
The Swede with the mystic right.

The Hart D

Man against horse, it has ever been so.
Who will win is always in doubt . . .
These contests take place at the rodeo,
In swirling dust, much grunting, and shout.

The luck of the draw determines the horse
Which the cowboy will mount for the fray.
The cowboy won't win lest he stays the course,
And the time of the whistle outstay.

An epic battle of grand proportion
Took place on the northern plain.
A cowboy in sync with bronco contortion,
Did for him, fame and glory attain.

As fate would have it, the man and the beast,
Were meant to meet in this struggle.
A rider of broncos, the man an artiste,
The bronc, riders objects to juggle.

The excitement grew high at word of the draw,
Young Brockway had drawn the Hart D.
That these two should meet was truly phenomena.
Who would win it was hard to foresee.

In all the north plain no horse was more feared
Than the Hart D, who was fearsome to buck.
Wild-eyed in demeanor and strangely crop-eared,
To ride no one had had any luck.

As the cowboy eased down on the Hart D's back,
The bronc quivered and got set to explode.
When they opened the chute on his rump they did whack,
He squealed rage at this pest to unload.

Bursting forth from the chute, he leaped for the sun,
His body both humping and twisting.
He was truly a sunfishing son-of-a-gun,
Every trick in his bag now enlisting.

But the rider sat tall and raked with each spur,
The legs, jabbing back on each side.
The action so swift, it all seemed a blur
Until Brockway finished that ride.

And so it was a hero was born:
The young rodeo star named Brockway.
He conquered Hart D and all blew his horn;
Of prowess, this truly his heyday.

Who Will Go?

"Who will go," was his cry, "my woman to save?"
As this mother-to-be lay there moaning.
"Save a doctor be had, she'll go to her grave,"
His fear-filled voice in high pitch now intoning.

Again came his plea, "Who will ride to the town?"
"I won't go," said the man from Dee Hollow.
"With wind howling fierce and snow swirling down,
In this darkness there's no trail one can follow."

"Won't you go, Rod Whipple, you've got a good horse,
You know the country much better than most?"
"Hey! It's thirty below," and without remorse,
He said, "No way, for my life comes foremost."

"Don't look at me!" said the quiet spoken Scot,
"Aye got me own wife and young ones to care for.
Mae duty to them cannot be unforgot,
Aye dare not risk seeing them never more."

Then Bart spoke with force all opinions to sway:
"No man alive could survive this fierce night.
Thirty miles in wild blizzard would end your day,
The frozen rider would ne'er again see the light."

Quiet fell o'er the room, each man searching his soul,
The young woman behind the curtain yet moaning.
It was then that Carl to his conscience console,
Said, "I'll go," his fear of dying disowning.

"I don't have a horse, who will lend me a horse?"
The brave Carl whispered to those gathered there.
"I'll lend you my horse; he'll do for the course,"
Said Rod Whipple, "if dangerous mission you dare."

Forward and onward through the blizzard he rode,
His only compass the fierce gale at his back.
Numbing cold and lostness did Carl cause forbode,
He'd need more than luck to keep true on the track.

At dawn's early light, Hallelujah his song,
For the horizon bared silouhette of the town.
As he breathed air of morn, joy of life surged strong,
A shining jewel would be now in his crown.

Rabbit Drive

They were sitting around laughing and talking
As farmers do on a cold winter day,
When one fellow said, "I was out walking;
Saw signs of rabbits everywhere on the way.

"The bounty hunters have killed off the coyotes,
I see their planes in the sky every day.
With predators gone and no antidotes,
Their population has now run away.

"If we don't take action they'll cause us damage
When crops and gardens come up in the spring.
What say a drive to destruction assuage?
We'll lessen damage for each rabbit we wing."

"That's real good suggestion," the farmers agreed,
"A rabbit drive is what we need for some fun.
It's so exciting when rabbits stampede,
To escape circle at sound of the gun."

"Takes two score of men," the first farmer said,
"Every man to be armed with a shotgun.
We'll walk to the middle from ten-mile spread,
From our stations will move forward as one."

On day of the drive excitement was rife
As each shooter was assigned to a station.
For avid hunters 'twas thrill of their life,
As their yearns turned to actualization.

At appointed time and all of one mind,
They moved forward each beating his can.
Startled rabbits jumped up, leaving shelters behind,
As mad flights toward the middle began.

Excitement built up as noose slowly tightened,
Both for hunter and for wild bounding hare.
Sensing the danger the hares now more frightened,
Created melee as they streaked here and there.

When signal was given the shooting began,
Forty shotguns did all blast and fire.
Fierce urge to kill made shooters barbarian,
Each intent that every rabbit expire.

In heat of massacre men too in danger,
When jack-rabbits made their dashes to flee.
The shooters then reckless would others endanger,
They'd swing and fire before hare could break free.

'Twas sad day for hare but good day for man,
For half a thousand were counted as killed.
Successful the drive as conceived by the plan,
Their goal freedom from hares now fulfilled.

Oka Romine

The story is told of a mystery man,
A large man who was handsome and lean.
About him was the air of a gentleman.
When asked his name, he said, "Oka Romine."

Where he had come from nobody knew;
Out of nowhere he appeared on the scene.
In warm days of August he made his debut,
The mystery stranger called Oka Romine.

This story they said happened long ago
In time of reaper and threshing machine.
On a day of threshing this man did show,
"I need some work," stated Oka Romine.

Both willing and able he bent hard to work;
The other threshers kept watching so keen.
Though hands soft and tender he didn't task shirk,
A hard worker was this Oka Romine.

On slack rainy day the crew lying around
Challenged stranger so aloof and serene.
In tests of strength he did locals astound,
They easily mastered by Oka Romine.

The maidens there about eyed him with favor;
Their flirting ways could by each one be seen,
But all were ignored without any waver
By the stranger they called Oka Romine.

One day without warning he asked for his pay,
From whence he came had never come clean.
He left as he came, mysterious his way,
The lone stranger they called Oka Romine.

He was last seen walking toward Canada,
When U.S. Marshals tried his path intervene.
A mass killer of women was wanted by law;
Could be the stranger known as Oka Romine.

Something to Think About

Without question, the greatest drama in a human life is facing death.

If one is unprepared for it, the fear of the unknown cannot help but bring apprehension and terror as one faces the big question, "What happens to me now?"

For the Christian it is quite another matter. The purpose of his faith and life has been to prepare him for this moment. He knows he is headed for the promised land and the words from the Twenty-third Psalm, "Yea, though I walk through the valley of the shadow of death, I will fear no evil for Thou art with me," is a source of great comfort. He knows that there will be a royal escort waiting to take him safely through to the other side.

Consequently, since death is inevitable and its time uncertain, wouldn't it be the height of folly to be unprepared when it comes?

For the procrastinators and the careless who plan to get serious about their salvation some day but aren't ready yet, let them be warned. The Bible declares in 2 Cor. 6:2, "Now is the day of salvation." Tomorrow will be too late if an unexpected death takes you today.

For those who are unbelievers, skeptics, or have been deceived by false Christs, it would be wise to rethink their positions and search the Scriptures for the truth.

The Bible states in Heb. 9:27, "It is appointed for man to die, and after that comes the judgment." That means there is no second chance. You have to be right the first time.

The Bible will reveal to you the way to be saved. In a way, it's like learning to swim. You have to get into the water in order to learn how. In the same way, you have to get into the word of God and believe what it says before you can learn how to be saved.

In John 3:16 it is stated, "God so loved the world that He gave his only begotten son, that whosoever believeth in him should not perish, but have everlasting life." As God gave his son for you, your part of the bargain is to receive him. In John 1:12, it is stated, "But to all who received him, who believed in his name, He gave power to become children of God."

This is where the comparison to learning how to swim comes into play. The act of receiving and believing is akin to getting into the water to learn how to swim. You have to receive and believe, after which God will give you power to become his children. You will then understand Acts 4:12 in which it says, "Salvation is found in no one else, for there is no other name under heaven given among men by which we must be saved."

A Holy God demands punishment for sin. The Christ willingly died on the cross to suffer that punishment. Your requirement is to repent and receive his sacrifice for you. To fail to do so means that you will have to suffer that punishment yourself, which is death, a fearsome price to pay. It's as simple as that.

The word "believe" is a giant word. Whether you do or don't believe in Jesus Christ and receive him as your Lord and Savior determines whether you will spend eternity in heaven or hell.

Does it not make sense that the mighty God who created this marvelous universe would have a plan to set up a kingdom of eternal righteousness, peace, and happiness and that in order to qualify for citizenship in that kingdom, you would have to meet the conditions laid down by his Son, The Lord Jesus Christ. Furthermore that this Christ proved by his resurrection from the dead that he has the power to deliver heaven after death to all believers. He is the only one in the history of the world claiming to be the Messiah who was resurrected from the dead. He is alive.

Remember, today is the day of salvation; tomorrow may be too late.

The Big Question

The big question will be who pays the price
At the end when you face the Almighty;
You and your works, or the Lord's sacrifice?
At stake is your place in eternity.

The answer of course, will be the lodestar,
You need to see and to understand.
For all will be guilty before the bar,
For perfection is the Father's demand.

For God in his wisdom when giving the law
Gave rules by which we should live.
Yet knowing our weakness He further foresaw
We would sin, and He'd need to forgive.

So God and the Son in heaven above
By their grace, they worked out a scheme.
They'd save fallen man by an act of love.
The Son would die on a cross to redeem.

So the Son was full perfect in keeping the laws
And fulfilled all the Father's demand;
He took on Himself all our character flaws,
To make us worthy for the glory land.

The result of it all is a matter of faith,
To accept what Christ did or reject.
Did He die for your sins, or is He only a wraith?
Choosing "yes" you'll become God's elect.

If yes be your answer, don't dilly dally,
For you might get hit by a truck.
Make your choice now, before in death's valley,
It would be folly to trust this to luck.

What Time Is It?

At the time of the ascension, as Jesus' disciples watched Him disappear into the clouds, two angels suddenly appeared to them. As written in Acts 1:11, they declared, "This same Jesus who has been taken from you into heaven will come back in the same way you have seen him go."

Ever since that time, mankind has been waiting for his second coming. Many have made ill-advised attempts to set dates for that event, but history records that not one has been right. This has added fuel to the fire of the skeptics. Peter foresaw that there would be scoffers in the last days and predicted by his statement in 2 Peter 3:4 that there would be those who would say, "Where is this coming he promised? Ever since our fathers died, everything goes on as it has since the beginning of creation." Peter, however, replied to such scoffing by saying that the Lord was not slow in keeping his promise, because he had a different way of keeping time. In 2 Peter 3:8, he said, "But do not forget this one thing, dear friends: With the Lord a day is like a thousand years, and a thousand years are like a day."

As recorded in Matthew 24:36, Jesus said, "No one knows the day or hour of his coming except the Father." However, Paul shed this light in 1 Thess. 5:4 "But ye, brethren, are not in darkness that that day should overtake you as a thief." Per Mark 13:28–31, Jesus declared, "Now learn this lesson from the fig tree. As soon as its twigs get tender and its leaves come out, you know that summer is near. Even so, when you see these things happening you know that it is near, right at the door. I tell you the truth, this generation will certainly not pass away until all these things have happened. Heaven and earth will pass away, but my words will never pass away." The interpreters tell us that the reference to the fig tree in the Bible means Israel, so is it not possible that her twigs got tender and leaves came out in the Year 1948 when she was reborn as a nation?

There is another important clue which may have significance in telling us where we stand in fulfillment of God's time chart. The number seven plays an important part in his scheme of things. In the first place, the story of creation in Genesis tells us God worked six days and then rested on the seventh. In Exodus 23:10 and 23:12, Moses revealed laws laid down by God for his people about the use of land and work. As to land, God said, "For six years you shall sow your land and gather in its yield, but the seventh year you shall let it rest and lie fallow." As to work, he commanded, "Six days you shall do your work, but on the seventh day you shall rest." The Apostle Paul further enlightens us in Hebrews 4:4

with the words, "For somewhere he has spoken about the seventh day in these words: And on the seventh day God rested from all his work."

Now if God applies this same principle for completing his plan for man on earth, he will finish his work in 6000 years, or 6 days, on the basis that 1000 days is as a day. Then will come the day of rest, another 1000 years, which fits exactly the millennium referred to in the Book of Revelation, which begins at Christ's return.

In the light of the above, the question to be asked is where are we now on God's clock. If the length of time from Adam to Christ is 4000 years, we will have completed the 6000 years around the year 2000 and God's six days of work will be done. Then Christ will come.

What time is it? In the face of the signs and the six day theory it is not out of the realm of possibility that the second hand is inching very close to that midnight hour. In Corinthians 15:52 the apostle Paul sounds the alert with the words, "In a flash, in the twinkling of an eye, at the last trumpet, for the trumpet will sound, the dead will be raised imperishable, and we will be changed." Could it be that that trumpeter in the sky even now has his trumpet out of the case and about to bring it to his lips?

Tick-Tock

Tick-tock, after the tock a second is shot,
Which for that moment is all time will allot.
As it slipped past beyond, where did it go?
In the march of history, it went to ago.

Tick-tock, sixty tocks and your minute is not.
That time which you had, you've no longer got.
When the ticks and tocks were in your preview
You knew, did you not, you can't time accrue.

Tick-tock, sixty minutes and now it's an hour,
The time machine working for time to devour.
Perhaps plenty of time to plant an oak tree,
To those who follow you'd leave as your legacy.

Tick-tock, twenty-four hours and sun sets again.
Of the day just spent, you'll say I recall when.
Was the time for the day well spent or lost?
Will the work that you did by reward be embossed?

Until time is no more, ticking-tocking won't end;
What's allotted each soul being their share to spend.
The days grow to months, and months into years,
As each milestone passes, one's time disappears.

When scripture was written, three score and ten,
Was the time allotted for each citizen;
Unless by reason of strength more time to receive,
A bonus to waste, or larger harvest to sheave.

At the time of rewards, they'll test all work;
This test by fire revealing good work or shirk.
Costly stone, gold, and silver will survive the test,
But hay, wood, and straw loss by fire you sufferest.

Have You?

Have you ever dreamed that you could fly,
To spread your wings and soar on high?
'Tis not a dream if you believe,
For when you die you'll wings receive.

Have you had visions of being rich
And with the wealthy find your niche?
Then don't store here but send above
Where you'll be rich by act of his love.

Have you had urge to see the world,
See flags of nations on poles unfurled?
I tell you, friend, set sight beyond;
You'll travel to stars with wave of wand.

Have you yearned for youth again,
Where limber limb you could regain?
Remember the promise of new body for you
In the land of forever where everything's new.

Have you longed for a better day
Where trials and burdens can't hold sway?
Don't let despond bar heaven's door,
For faith will open and joy restore.

Have you wished for love of a friend
No matter what, on whom to depend?
The Good Book tells of the family of God
Where his sons are closer than peas in pod.

Have you been sorry for your sin
Where prick of conscience lies therein?
Forgiveness starts at confession's door
Where God forgives you forevermore.

Have you hungered for the love of God,
When He'll deliver like Aaron's rod?
Behold! He stands at your door to knock;
He'll enter your heart if door you unlock.

.